Contents

A Personal Statement from the Prime Minister

10 DOWNING STREET
LONDON SW1A 2AA

THE PRIME MINISTER

This government was elected on a promise of change. A promise to create a new and modern Britain for the 21st century. That is what we pledged to do. And we are delivering.

Step by step that change is happening and Britain is becoming a better place to live in. But it could be so much better if we could break once and for all the vicious cycle of drugs and crime which wrecks lives and threatens communities.

The fight against drugs should be part of a wider range of policies to renew our communities and ensure decent opportunities are available to all.

We are tackling inequalities through the largest ever programme to get people off benefit and into work and a series of reforms in the welfare state, education, health, criminal justice and the economy.

But that is not enough. I am determined to tackle the drugs problem. That is why I appointed Keith Hellawell as the first ever UK Anti-Drugs Coordinator to put together a comprehensive strategy, coming at the problem afresh.

This strategy is an important step forward in developing a cooperative approach. But the fight is not just for the Government. It is for teachers, parents, community groups, those working in the field and everyone who cares about the future of our society. We owe it to our children to come up with a truly imaginative solution and create the better Britain they deserve.

Tony Blair

The Government's Ten-Year Strategy for Tackling Drugs

Ann Taylor

John Prescott

Gordon Brown

Robin Cook

Jack Straw

David Blunkett

Donald Dewar

Frank Dobson

Mo Mowlam

Ron Davies

THE PROBLEM

Drugs are a very serious problem in the UK. No one has any illusions about that. Illegal drugs are now more widely available than ever before and children are increasingly exposed to them. Drugs are a threat to health, a threat on the streets and a serious threat to communities because of drug-related crime.

Some progress has been made. The last Government's strategy for England "Tackling Drugs Together" was an important step in the right direction. It has been implemented with some success. For the first time, Drug Action Teams set up partnerships to tackle the problem. We will build on that valuable work. But a fresh long-term approach is now needed.

VISION

There are no easy answers. To really make a difference in tackling drugs, goals must be long term. Our new vision is to create a healthy and confident society, increasingly free from the harm caused by the misuse of drugs. Our approach combines firm enforcement with prevention.

Drug problems do not occur in isolation. They are often tied in with other social problems. The Government is tackling inequalities through the largest ever programme to get people off benefit and into work and a series of reforms in the welfare state, education, health, criminal justice and the economy. And a new Social Exclusion Unit is looking at many of the problems often associated with drug taking.

The Government will promote action against drugs that makes substantial progress over the long term. Action will be concentrated in areas of greatest need and risk. All drugs are harmful and enforcement against all illegal substances will continue. And we will focus on those that cause the greatest damage, including heroin and cocaine.

Partnership is the key to the new approach, building on the good work that has already been done. This strategy is based on an extensive review by the UK Anti-Drugs Coordinator, Keith Hellawell and his Deputy, Mike Trace. They analysed all the available evidence and together consulted over 2,000 people and organisations.

The strategy has four elements:

1   **YOUNG PEOPLE** - to help young people resist drug misuse in order to achieve their full potential in society;

2   **COMMUNITIES** - to protect our communities from drug-related anti-social and criminal behaviour;

3   **TREATMENT** - to enable people with drug problems to overcome them and live healthy and crime-free lives;

4   **AVAILABILITY** - to stifle the availability of illegal drugs on our streets.

This is a framework for designing and implementing policies to tackle drugs. It is just the beginning of a long-term strategy.

In the first year of the strategy, clear, consistent and rigorous targets will be set to help achieve our aims. The performance of the Government and its agencies therefore will be readily measurable against these targets. And the UK Anti-Drugs Coordinator will publish an annual report to check progress.

PARTNERSHIP

Because of the complexity of the problem, partnership really is essential at every level. At government level, the work will be led by the Cabinet Sub-Committee on Drug Misuse chaired by Ann Taylor and by other groups chaired by Keith Hellawell and his Deputy Mike Trace.

These will bring together key players in the field from the statutory, voluntary and private sectors and others with an interest. They will work closely with the local partnerships set up by Drug Action Teams. The Drug Action Teams are the critical link in the chain, ensuring that this strategy is translated into concrete action. To assist in that, detailed guidance notes are being issued to those working in the field putting this strategy into practice.

RESOURCES

In central and local government alone, well over £1 billion a year is spent on tackling the drugs problem. And yet the number of addicts is going up and availability and drug-related crime are on the increase. We need to improve the efficiency and coordination of anti-drugs work. And eventually, we hope to achieve better results. If we invest wisely now, there is a real chance of breaking the cycle of drugs and crime which wrecks lives and threatens communities. Along with the obvious benefits of creating a healthier society, there could also be significant savings through big reductions in crime and health risks.

To achieve that, all government departments have committed themselves to the principles guiding the allocation of resources described in Keith Hellawell's report. There will be a progressive shift away from reactive expenditure, dealing with the consequences of drug misuse, to positive investment in helping prevent them ever arising. The Coordinator's report takes into account work currently being done on the comprehensive spending review of drugs-related spending which will be completed later this year. And for the first time, a proportion of assets seized from drug barons will be channelled back into anti-drug programmes to help those who have suffered at their hands and on whose misfortune they have prospered. The Government is considering how this can best be achieved. More details of these considerations will be issued later this year.

THE WAY AHEAD

The strategy is a challenging work programme to which all relevant agencies will need to respond. Work must be properly coordinated. The Government will make clear what it expects from its key agencies with an interest - police forces and authorities, probation committees, prison establishments, health authorities, local authorities (including Directors of Education and Social Services), HM Customs and Excise, the National Crime Squad and the National Criminal Intelligence Service. Similarly, with Drug Action Teams.

Although the strategy focuses mainly on England, it is relevant to Scotland, Wales and Northern Ireland and it highlights our international responsibilities. We will make sure it gets the widest circulation. And our international effort remains vitally important, working with our European and other partners, to stem the flow of illegal drugs into the UK.

The legal framework provided by the Misuse of Drugs Act 1971 and other legislation provides some of the tools needed to crack down on the availability of drugs and reduce the misery they cause. But enforcement alone will never be enough. We need to ensure that young people have all the information they need to make informed decisions about drugs; that we follow up tough words with decisive action; and that there really is proper partnership to tackle the problem. If we can make our vision a reality, we have the chance to make Britain a better place. This new strategy presents a real opportunity to do that.

THE GOVERNMENT'S ANTI-DRUGS STRATEGY: OUTLINE

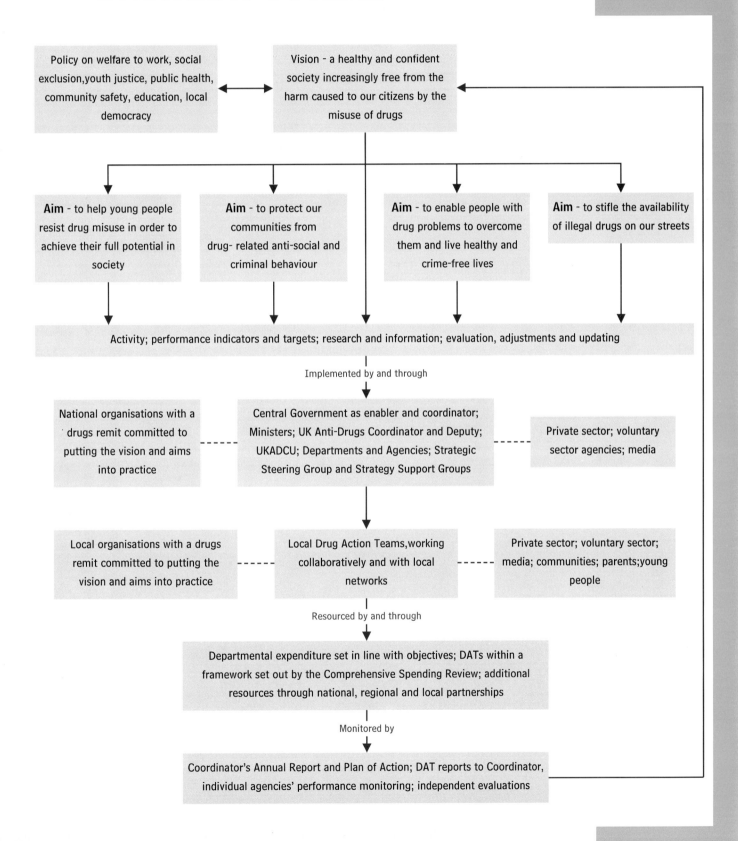

Policy on welfare to work, social exclusion, youth justice, public health, community safety, education, local democracy

Vision - a healthy and confident society increasingly free from the harm caused to our citizens by the misuse of drugs

Aim - to help young people resist drug misuse in order to achieve their full potential in society

Aim - to protect our communities from drug- related anti-social and criminal behaviour

Aim - to enable people with drug problems to overcome them and live healthy and crime-free lives

Aim - to stifle the availability of illegal drugs on our streets

Activity; performance indicators and targets; research and information; evaluation, adjustments and updating

Implemented by and through

National organisations with a drugs remit committed to putting the vision and aims into practice

Central Government as enabler and coordinator; Ministers; UK Anti-Drugs Coordinator and Deputy; UKADCU; Departments and Agencies; Strategic Steering Group and Strategy Support Groups

Private sector; voluntary sector agencies; media

Local organisations with a drugs remit committed to putting the vision and aims into practice

Local Drug Action Teams, working collaboratively and with local networks

Private sector; voluntary sector; media; communities; parents; young people

Resourced by and through

Departmental expenditure set in line with objectives; DATs within a framework set out by the Comprehensive Spending Review; additional resources through national, regional and local partnerships

Monitored by

Coordinator's Annual Report and Plan of Action; DAT reports to Coordinator, individual agencies' performance monitoring; independent evaluations

REPORT OF THE UK ANTI-DRUGS COORDINATOR

INTRODUCTION

I share the Government's vision for the future - a healthy and confident society increasingly free from the harm caused by the misuse of drugs.

To achieve this we must all combine to:

- address the social issues which contribute to young people, in particular, becoming attracted to drug taking;

- bolster and support those who wish to help and guide them;

- provide sufficient services to treat those who have drugs problems;

- concentrate our international and law enforcement effort on those who produce, process, distribute and sell them;

- develop a criminal justice system which deals effectively both with those who appear before it for greed and for need.

The focus of this document is on illegal drugs as determined by the Misuse of Drugs Act 1971. However it is clear to me that legally obtainable substances such as alcohol, tobacco, solvents and prescribed drugs used without medical control have close links with illegal drugs problems and should therefore be addressed, as appropriate, within the strategy.

Drug misuse in the late 1990s poses many problems for our society. Research suggests that there are all kinds of reasons for misuse; that key factors include unemployment, low self esteem, educational failure, boredom and physical, psychological or family problems. Even where the cause relates more to experimentation or enjoyment, or to a shift from alcohol or tobacco, the fact is that overtly mind-altering substances have greater pull than other activities. And many people misuse drugs because they don't have the opportunity to lead fulfilling lives.

The consequences of drug activity include serious and organised crime; wide-spread acquisitive crime for drug addicts funding their habit; violence generated by drug intoxication and dealers; and hidden social problems - in homes and schools, on the roads and in the workplace.

The social, economic, psychological, crime and health-related costs are formidable. The latest Government-funded research suggests that annual costs arising from the most serious drug misusers alone are **well over £4 billion**.

Significant health risks are associated with drugs - the more evidence that becomes available about the risks of, for example, cannabis and ecstasy, the more discredited the notion that any of the substances currently controlled under the 1971 Act are harmless.

But there are many misconceptions. All young people do **not** take drugs; all drug takers are **not** addicts; all drugs do **not** kill; all drug takers do **not** commit crime; illegal drugs are **not** the unique preserve of people from particular social or ethnic backgrounds.

The majority of people in this country **do not nor have ever** taken an illegal substance; and the majority of those who have are experimenters or casual users. A majority of illegal drug users do so for so-called "recreational purposes". By far the minority of illegal drug users - between 100,000 and 200,000 people[1] - become addicts. It is this group which causes the greatest problem for society and themselves. They are responsible for a substantial amount of crime; many are victims of abuse from drug dealers and pimps; they are often disruptive and make disproportionate demands on law enforcement, medical, counselling and social services. The response to this group has so far been patchy. Although individuals and agencies are working very hard within their own area, they are trying to achieve progress against inconsistencies within the operation of the criminal justice system; inadequate treatment and prescribing facilities; haphazard funding arrangements which have a bias towards reacting rather than preventing; and a paucity of timely and consistent information. It is crucial that we learn from the past and adopt a consistent approach in the future.

I believe that the four aims of helping young people, protecting communities, enabling those with problems to overcome them and stifling availability of drugs will allow us all to channel our efforts towards significant improvements over time. I believe that over the next ten years we should be looking to achieve significant reductions in young people's drug use and drug-related offending; an increase in the participation of problem drug misusers in treatment programmes;and reductions in the availability of drugs. In our progress towards these aims it is essential that we monitor the effectiveness of our individual and collective activities in an objective way. We need also to set about achieving our corporate and single agency targets on an annual basis and monitoring our progress in reaching them. Much work will need to be done within the next twelve months to develop these targets in relation to the activities outlined in each section of this report.

The focus of this first report is on England, but I would expect all other parts of the UK to reflect on the implications of this strategy for them and report back on relevant developments by February 1999.

By March 1999:

- all agencies should realign their priorities, resources and operational focus in line with this White Paper and produce their forward plan;

- all agencies should develop corporate and individual performance targets and measures;

- national, local, private and voluntary sector funding should be realigned in support of the plan;

- I will publish my first Annual Report and Plan of Action Against Drugs.

---

1. "Arrest Referral – Emerging lessons from research" – Edmunds M et al (1998)

This process will be repeated every year. It will be influenced by experience, research, evaluation, changes in patterns of drug misuse, successes and failures at national, corporate and individual level. Every three years, we need to have a systematic and comprehensive appraisal of the strategy's impact based on independent evaluations, and adjust the way forward accordingly. The importance of rigorous evaluation cannot be overstated.

In tackling the drugs problem, we must now shift our emphasis from reacting to the consequences of drug misuse to tackling its root causes. This should be reflected in Government financial programmes. The challenge is to protect the young and vulnerable, offer alternatives to the disaffected, stop those who flout the rules, and arrest and imprison those who profit from the drugs trade.

There are a great many talented and committed people working in the field. I want to see them really working together. I want them to be free from obstacles which stop them doing that effectively now. Action against drugs should be at the heart of government policy. Working together we can make an impact in schools, colleges, universities, on the streets, in the workplace and in our homes. There is now a unique opportunity to invest in the future. We must not squander it.

Keith Hellawell

THE DRUGS PROBLEM: WHERE WE ARE NOW

"Tackling Drugs Together", published in May 1995, was the first genuinely strategic response in England to the complexities of the drugs problem. It had cross-Party support and has been successful in sustaining a coordinated approach to a difficult issue. The fact that all 88 of the tasks required in that White Paper have been completed indicates good progress. It remains one of the best and most influential strategies for effective action against drugs. But in building on its success, we need to recognise its weaknesses:

- it focused on structures rather than results, with the general public insufficiently engaged as a consequence;

- it treated drug misuse largely in isolation from other social and environmental factors;

- it advocated partnership without making sufficient structural and fiscal changes to support it;

- it was too short-term and did not bring together common research, information and performance bases.

Alongside **"Tackling Drugs Together"**, there have been other important developments:

- A strategic review of **international drugs activity** - with a clear overall commitment of all the law enforcement, intelligence and diplomatic agencies to reduce the flow of illicit drugs to the UK.

- **Strengthened links** between a wide range of national agencies, working together to achieve collaborative goals on drug prevention/education and enforcement - an approach which has been confirmed by recent reports from the statutory Inspectorates on the Police, Probation, Prisons, Education and Social Services.

- Increased **collaboration on resources** between the statutory, private and voluntary sectors - for example, the £2 million drugs Challenge Fund in 1996/7 and 1997/8 respectively has generated a total of over £2.5 million resources from those sectors.

- The creation and development of **Drug Action Teams** and their Reference Groups which has been very encouraging, with substantially greater cohesion of effort and sharing of resources amongst health and local authorities, criminal justice agencies and other key players, agreed action plans and better prioritisation of local needs.

- Community initiatives which have generated a diverse range of projects, clearly highlighting that local people are best placed to tackle local drugs problems. Evidence of this has been disseminated, in particular by the Home Office **Drugs Prevention Initiative**.

Significant progress too has been made in **Scotland, Wales and Northern Ireland**:

● in **Scotland**, the 1994 strategy "Drugs in Scotland: meeting the challenge" has been implemented, along with the development of the Scotland Against Drugs campaign and a Scottish drugs Challenge Fund. The emphasis has been on an integrated approach to service provision, the development of a national information base and strong partnership links with the private and voluntary sectors;

● in **Wales**, a drug and alcohol strategy "Forward Together" was launched in 1996. The Welsh Drug and Alcohol Unit oversees the strategy, and is committed to developing a national prevention campaign, action on treatment and rehabilitation, and guidance for those involved in combatting drug and alcohol misuse;

● in **Northern Ireland**, the Central Coordinating Group for Action Against Drugs was established in 1995 to oversee coherent efforts against drug misuse within a clearly defined policy statement. The key action areas are education and prevention, treatment and rehabilitation, law enforcement, information and research - including a major publicity campaign - and monitoring and evaluation.

The scale of the problem

Despite this progress, the drugs problem remains formidable. For example:

● record levels of drug seizures reveal the increasing threat of a widening range of trafficking routes to the UK, against a background of expanding global production;

● offenders dealt with under the Misuse of Drug Act 1971 are up from 86,000 in 1994 to 95,000 in 1996;

● 48% of 16-24 year olds questioned in 1996 had ever used illegal drugs compared with 45% in 1994 (and 18% had used in the last month, compared with 17% in 1994);

● the number of drug misusers attending services was 24,879 in the six month period ending September 1996, 48% higher than the equivalent period three years earlier;

● the number of deaths in the UK attributable to the misuse of drugs has risen from 1,399 in 1993 to 1,805 in 1995.

In addition, more localised trends - particularly the increasing availability and use of cheap, smokeable heroin - suggest growing exposure and consumption by increasingly younger people.

THE UNDERLYING PRINCIPLES OF THE STRATEGY

Integration. Drug problems do not occur in isolation. They are often tied in with other social problems. The Government is tackling inequalities through the largest-ever programme to get people off benefit and into work and a series of reforms in the welfare state, education, health, criminal justice and the economy. And a new Social Exclusion Unit is looking at many of the problems often associated with drug taking such as school exclusions, truancy, rough sleeping and poor housing. It is important to remember these connections, and that key results in other areas of activity, such as general take-up rates for further and higher education and employment, relate clearly to the development of this strategy.

Evidence. Drug misuse can be a highly-charged subject. Learning about an illicit activity can be difficult but our strategy must be based on accurate, independent research, approached in a level-headed, analytical fashion.

Joint Action. Partnership is not an end in itself, and can be an excuse for blurring responsibilities and inactivity. But the evidence is that joint action - if managed effectively - has a far greater impact on the complex drugs problem than disparate activities.

Consistency of Action. While activities must relate to local circumstances and priorities, drugs misuse is a national problem requiring fairness and consistency in our response.

Effective Communication. We need to be clear and consistent in the messages we send to young people and to society – in particular, the importance of reinforcing at every opportunity that drug-taking can be harmful.

Accountability. Through the Coordinator's Annual Report and Plan of Action Against Drugs, we can dispassionately and objectively track progress. The structures, resources and performance mechanisms set out in this report exist solely for that purpose, so that we can be sure our achievements are real. A special focus will be given to the four key objectives identified below - one for each aim.

AIM (i): Young People - To Help Young People Resist Drug Misuse in Order to Achieve Their Full Potential in Society

Young people, and those responsible for them, need to be prepared both to resist drugs and, as necessary, to handle drug-related problems. Information, skills and support need to be provided in ways which are sensitive to age and circumstances, and particular efforts need to be made to reach and help those groups at high risk of developing very serious problems. Prevention should start early, with broad life-skills approaches at primary school, and built on over time with appropriate programmes for young people as they grow older via youth work, peer approaches, training and wider community support. The aim is for approaches to be better integrated nationally and locally.

● ## Key objective

Reduce proportion of people under 25 reporting use of illegal drugs in the last month and previous year.

● ## Drugs and young people: the facts

We now know a great deal about the relationship between drugs and young people. Many never take drugs at all, many who do experiment grow out of it quickly, but a small hardcore develop very serious problems. In particular:

● drugs misuse is most common amongst people in their teens and early twenties, but the average age of first drug use is becoming younger;[2]

● almost half of young people are likely to take drugs at some time in their lives, but only about one-fifth will become regular misusers, (ie at least once a month), with a tiny minority of that group taking drugs on a daily basis;[2]

● most young people who take drugs do so out of curiosity, boredom, or peer pressure - and continue misusing drugs through a combination of factors ranging from enjoyment to physical and psychological dependency;

● cannabis is easily the most commonly-used drug amongst the young, followed by amphetamines, poppers, LSD and ecstasy[2] - while there are some identifiable groups such as cannabis users , dance drug users and addicts, the trend is towards more indiscriminate use, based on price and availability;

● there is a very strong correlation between the use of illegal drugs and the use of volatile substances, tobacco and alcohol amongst young people;

● there is increasingly strong evidence that the earlier a young person starts taking drugs, the greater the chance that he or she will develop serious drugs problems over time;

● for early to mid-teenagers, there are strong links between drugs problems, exclusion or truancy from school, break-up of the family, and initiation into criminal activity;

● for older teenagers and people in their twenties, there are strong links between drugs problems and unemployment, homelessness, prostitution and other features of social exclusion;

● whatever other influences affect young people, the role of parents throughout this process is crucial.

2. "Drug Misuse Declared in 1996: Key Results from the British Crime Survey" – Ramsay M and Spiller J. Home Office Research Findings No 56 (1997)

Programme of action

All activity supported by this stategy will:

- inform young people, parents, and those who advise/work with them about the risks and consequences of drug misuse, linked to other substances - including alcohol, tobacco and solvents - where appropriate;

- teach young people from the age of five upwards - both in and out of formal education settings - the skills needed to resist pressure to misuse drugs, including a more integrated approach to Personal Social and Health Education in schools, and with particular reference to the forthcoming 1998 DfEE guidance;

- help make the misuse of drugs less culturally acceptable to young people, including the use of effective and targeted national and local publicity and information;

- promote healthy lifestyles and positive activities not involving drugs and other substance misuse;

- ensure that the groups of young people most at risk of developing serious drugs problems receive appropriate and specific interventions;

- ensure that young people from all backgrounds, whatever their culture, gender or race, have access to appropriate programmes;

- build on and disseminate good practice in identifying what works best in prevention and education activity.

Assessment

Performance indicators for each of these activities will be introduced to monitor achievement and specific targets set for agencies against the following objectives:

- reduce proportion of people under 25 reporting use of illegal drugs in the last month and previous year - **KEY OBJECTIVE**;

- increase levels of knowledge of 5-16 year olds about risks and consequences of drug misuse;

- delay age of first use of illegal drugs;

- reduce exclusions from schools arising from drug-related incidents;

- reduce the number of people under 25 using heroin;

- increase access to information and services for vulnerable groups - including school excludees, truants, looked after children, young offenders, young homeless and children of drug-misusing parents.

Research and Information

To support these objectives we will make use of the best available sources of information and plan as a priority to commission additional research as follows:

● comprehensive surveys of young people (age 5 upwards) and drugs misuse;

● qualitative studies of patterns of misuse of regular young users;

● long-term evaluations of effectiveness of prevention and education programmes;

● qualitative and long-term assessment of impact on drug misuse of wider social factors;

● operational summary of effective prevention and education.

Aim (ii): Communities - To protect our Communities from Drug-Related Anti-Social and Criminal Behaviour

Helping drug-misusing offenders to tackle their drug problems and become better integrated into society has a significant impact on levels of crime. Local partnerships can work successfully to tackle local drug problems, and to improve the quality of life for communities.

● Key objective

Reduce levels of repeat offending amongst drug misusing offenders.

● Drugs and the communities: the facts

Drugs and crime are of concern to all communities, particularly drug possession, manufacture and trafficking, the involvement of criminal syndicates in the drugs trade, the acquisitive crime committed by drug misusing offenders to feed their habits, and the anti-social behaviour and feeling of menace that the drug culture generates within neighbourhoods. It is very clear that effective enforcement under the 1971 Act remains vital to minimising the availability of drugs and the threats to the community that the drug culture carries in its wake. The criminal justice system operates with considerable discretion within this framework but we must guard against this resulting in inconsistencies. The growing clarity of the relationship between drugs and crime has highlighted that:

● many police forces estimate that around half of all recorded crime has some drug related element to it, whether in terms of individual consumption or supply of drugs, or the consequent impact of it on criminal behaviour;

● a small number of people are responsible for huge numbers of crimes - 664 addicts surveyed committed 70,000 offences over a three month period;[3]

● latest indications from a random sample of suspected offenders arrested by the police suggest that over 60% of arrestees have traces of illegal drugs in their urine;[4]

● emerging evidence suggests that effective and targeted treatment for drug misusing offenders can have a major impact on reducing subsequent offending;[3]

● the general costs to the criminal justice system of drug-related crime are, at a very conservative estimate, at least £1 billion every year;[5]

● community safety partnerships - which target specific drugs problems in the community - such as disrupting visible markets, drugs in pubs and clubs, drugs in the workplace and drugs and driving - have great potential where the approach taken is locally based, properly resourced, consistently delivered and long-term.

3. "National Treatment Outcome Research Study. Summary of the project, the clients and preliminary findings." – Gossop M. NTORS (1996)
4. "Drug Testing Arrestees, Home Office Research Findings". No 70 – Bennett T. (1998)
5. Preliminary results from Drugs Comprehensive Spending Review.

Programme of Action

All activity supported by this strategy will:

- develop sustained and collaborative treatment for those committing drug-related crime - including support for the piloting of Drug Treatment and Testing Orders, promotion of Caution Plus schemes (according to Home Office and ACPO guidelines) and associated projects within existing legislation, ensuring that their lessons are spread and implemented as widely as possible;

- target police resources on the detection of drug-related crime and refer offenders where appropriate;

- provide visible deterrence and public reassurance through the consistent punishment of drug dealers and suppliers, and the disruption of their markets;

- ensure community support in achieving a consistent application of the drugs laws, including compatibility in dealing with low level possession offences amongst different prosecution agencies;

- energise and involve local communities through collaborative responses to local drug problems - with imaginative use of existing and planned community safety/estate action/drug network partnerships - so that positive outcomes, focused on the drugs and the people that cause most damage and danger, are achieved;

- increase take-up rate of further education and employment by former addicted criminals through welfare to work, New Deal and other means;

- tackle drugs in clubs in line with recent Home Office guidance;

- implement drugs in the workplace initiatives in line with Health and Safety Executive guidance for employers;

- enhance detection and underline the social unacceptability of driving while influenced by drugs.

Assessment

Performance indicators for each of these activities will be introduced to monitor achievement and specific targets set for agencies against the following objectives:

- reduce levels of repeat offending amongst drug misusing offenders - **KEY OBJECTIVE**;

- increase the number of offenders referred to and entering treatment programmes as a result of arrest referral schemes, the court process and post-sentencing provision;

- reduce levels of crime committed to pay for drug misuse;

- reduce drugs market places that are of particular concern to local communities;

- reduce levels of drug-related absenteeism/dismissals from work;

- reduce numbers of road deaths and injuries where drugs are a contributory factor.

Research and Information

To support these objectives we will make use of the best available sources of information and plan as a priority to commission additional research as follows:

- long-term evaluations of community safety programmes within high risk communities;

- further assessment of cost-effective treatment in the criminal justice system;

- practices that have led to sustained reductions in drug-related crime and community fear; and

- studies into the links between drug misuse and absenteeism, and between drugs and road deaths.

AIM (iii): Treatment - To Enable People With Drug Problems to Overcome them and Live Healthy and Crime-free Lives

Many of those with the most serious drugs problems have a range of other problems, including lack of housing or employment. We will ensure that specific, appropriate and timely help is provided to those with drug problems and that their needs are recognised and addressed by wider Government programmes.

● Key objective

Increase participation of problem drug misusers, including prisoners, in drug treatment programmes which have a positive impact on health and crime.

● Drug treatment: the facts

There is growing evidence that treatment works. In particular, harm reduction work over the last 15 years has had a major impact on the rate of HIV and other drug-related infections. And rehabilitation programmes have shown real gains in crime reduction. The rate of demand for treatment services amongst seriously dependent drug misusers shows no sign of abating, and the supply of effective treatment services is failing to match that demand. In particular:

● the number of addicts has risen steadily - there were 38,000 people notified in England as drug addicts in 1996, compared with 22,000 in 1992;[6]

● the total number of seriously problematic drug misusers in this country is estimated to be between 100,000 and 200,000, many of whom do not seek or cannot get access to effective services;[7]

● the scope, accessibility and effectiveness of available treatments are inconsistent between localities and generally insufficient. There is considerable insecurity about funding and disparity in provision. Consequently, there is rarely immediate access for a drug misuser to a treatment programme - given the urgency of the needs of most drug misusers, this is unacceptable. The Department of Health report "The Task Force to Review Services for Drug Misusers" (1996) points a clear way forward for developing effective treatment provision in this country - as does the Health Advisory Service report on "Children and Young People – Substance Misuse Services" (1996) with respect to services to adolescents. The challenge is to put the recommendations of these two reports firmly into practice;

● the most significant health risks for this group beyond drug dependency are HIV, hepatitis B and C, and a wide range of psychiatric and psychological problems. Drug related deaths - proportionately rare but probably under-reported - are increasing. Injecting, however, appears to be continuing its fall, with only 2 in 5 addicts now admitting ever injecting;[8]

● there is increasing evidence of the links between health problems of individual drug misusers and public health concerns - notably mental health problems, alcohol abuse and tobacco use, and social exclusion.

● Programme of Action

All activity supported by this strategy will:

● ensure all problem drug misusers - irrespective of age, gender, race and drug with which they have a problem - have proper access to support from appropriate

6. Statistics of Drug Addicts Notified to the Home Office, United Kingdom, 1996 – Corkery JM (1997)
7. "Arrest Referral – Emerging lessons from research" – Edmunds M et al(1998)
8. Drug Misuse Statistics for six months ending September 1996 – Department of Health (1998)

services - including primary care - when needed, providing specific support services for young people, ethnic minorities, women and their babies;

● provide problem drug misusers with accurate information, advice and practical help to avoid infections and other health problems related to their misuse;

● support problem drug misusers in reviewing and changing their behaviour towards more positive lifestyles - linking up where appropriate with accommodation, education and employment services;

● provide an integrated, effective and efficient response to people with drugs and mental health problems;

● ensure that prescription of substitute medications (eg methadone) in particular and dispensing of clinical services in general (including prescribed legal drugs) are in line with forthcoming Department of Health clinical guidelines;

● improve the range and quality of treatment services provision specifically for the under 25s, in line with Standing Conference on Drug Abuse guidance;

● ensure that throughcare and aftercare arrangements for drug misusing prisoners are coherent, focused and linked to community provision;

● develop collaborative, coherent, accessible and cost-effective service provision through Drug Action Teams.

Assessment

Performance indicators for each of these activities will be introduced to monitor achievement and specific targets set for agencies against the following objectives:

● increase participation of problem drug misusers, including prisoners, in drug treatment programmes which have a positive impact on health and crime - **KEY OBJECTIVE**;

● increase the proportion of problem drug misusers in contact with drugs services;

● reduce the proportion of drug misusers who inject, and the proportion of those sharing injecting equipment over previous three months;

● reduce numbers of drug-related deaths;

● reduce numbers of drug misusers being denied immediate access to appropriate treatment.

Research and Information

To support these objectives we will make use of the best available sources of information and plan as a priority to commission additional research as follows:

- the clinical and social care of people with drugs and mental health problems;

- the cost-effectiveness of current treatment and care options;

- the effectiveness of treatment interventions for young people;

- the lessons from the Advisory Council on the Misuse of Drugs study of drug-related deaths;

- the links between recreational drug misuse (including cannabis) and later health problems;

- the treatment of stimulant drug dependency.

AIM (iv): Availability - To stifle the Availability of Illegal Drugs on our Streets

Constant vigilance is needed to tackle availability where it matters most, close to home. It is crucial to gain a better understanding of which activities have the most impact on local availability and to pursue them, improving partnership between agencies along the way.

● **Key objective**

Reduce access to drugs amongst 5-16 year olds.

● **The drugs trade: the facts**

The drugs trade is an international multi-billion pound industry. A 1997 report by the UN Drug Control Programme estimates that the industry's turnover amounts to about 8% of total international trade, approximately the same as textiles, oil, gas or world tourism. The threat is ever present and growing. And, however impressive the enforcement activity in general, there have been no signs of street level availability reducing over recent years. The facts are:

● the routes into the UK for heroin and cocaine have become increasingly complex, but remain primarily, for heroin, the Golden Crescent through Turkey and the Balkan route and, for cocaine, South America and the Caribbean - over half of all seizures arrive in the UK via other EU countries;

● the routes for synthetic drugs have been characterised by heavy ecstasy production in the Netherlands and increasing flows of manufactured drugs from Eastern Europe;

● the UK is primarily an importer of drugs. Domestic production, although limited, is increasing.

● proven cases of internal corruption within enforcement agencies are few, but the threat is real and requires constant vigilance;

● the impact on street level availability of activity against supplies is difficult to assess and the price of drugs within the UK has generally shown a stable or downward trend. However, there is a marked difference between the price of drugs here and in source and transit countries - for example, heroin is sold at £850 per kg in Pakistan, £7,000 in Turkey, £15,300 in the Netherlands and £24,000 in the UK, which then translates into £72,000 on our streets. There is therefore evidence to suggest that effective enforcement is a factor in pushing up those prices;

● the direct impact of enforcement on short term availability is difficult to establish. There is, however, Home Office research evidence which suggests that focused and coordinated activity on local drug markets can make a significant and sustained impact on availability, reducing supplies, pushing prices up and reducing the threat of exposure of young people to drugs;

● the drugs trade also includes significant quantities of drugs which have been legally manufactured and then leaked on to the illicit market, primarily via the prescription system.

Programme of Action

All activity supported by this strategy will:

- reduce the acreage of drug crops produced and the amounts processed; control the illicit supply of chemicals and materials used in production and manufacture of drugs; and control the movement of drugs from producer to processing countries;

- raise the commitment and effectiveness of interdiction efforts in countries which pose a threat of drug supplies to the UK;

- reduce the amount of drugs coming to and crossing the UK borders through seizures and by dismantling or disrupting trafficking organisations;

- reduce the growth, manufacture and distribution of drugs within the UK, preventing them from reaching local dealers through seizures and by dismantling or disrupting internal networks;

- target money launderers and increase the amount of assets confiscated and recovered from drug activities;

- reduce levels of street dealing and the availability of drugs in communities;

- reduce the availability of drugs within prisons;

- ensure full cooperation and collaboration, at every level, amongst the enforcement and intelligence agencies, with the focus clearly on tackling activity which causes the most damage to local communities

The respective roles and responsibilities of the police and HM Customs and Excise are well defined. Within that framework, the creation of the National Crime Squad as of 1st April 1998 will enhance the effectiveness of the police service. During 1998/99 we shall look at how the objectives of the various agencies engaged in stifling availability can be further coordinated to secure increased effectiveness.

Assessment

Performance indicators for each of these activities will be introduced to monitor achievement and specific targets set for agencies against the following objectives:

- reduce access to drugs amongst 5-16 year olds - **KEY OBJECTIVE**;

- increase the effectiveness of the overseas diplomatic and operational effort;

- increase the value of illegal drugs seized and/or prevented from entering or distributed within the UK;

- increase the number of trafficking groups disrupted or dismantled;

- increase the numbers of offenders dealt with for supply offences;

- increase the amount of assets identified, and the proportion confiscated and recovered from drug trafficking and money laundering;

- reduce prisoner access to drugs.

Research and Information

To support these objectives we will make use of the best available sources of information and plan as a priority to commission additional research as follows:

- harness all the information gathering agencies, both within our control and those with whom we have influence, to produce a common data model which has strategic as well as operational benefits;

- establish the quantity, quality and type of drugs reaching our streets; its place of origin, distribution network and means of transport; and the most effective methods of intervention at each stage of the process;

- establish the quantity and type of precursor chemical manufactured, its place of origin, its destination and its route of passage;

- establish an objective base for the level of assets and money associated with the drug industry mapping the agencies and individual concerned;

- establish the relationship between street level prices, availability and demand.

RESOURCING AND MANAGING THE WORK

For the strategy to be effective, clarity about the delivery mechanisms - the structures, resources, responsibilities, accountability and basis for audit and evaluation - is essential.

UK Coordination

Genuine collaboration across Government is the driving force behind this strategy. The role of individual departments, agencies and the voluntary and private sectors is to contribute to the overall vision and aims, in addition to their own specific tasks. The Cabinet sub-Committee on Drug Misuse - known as HS(D) - will be the Ministerial body responsible for ensuring that this occurs.

The UK Anti-Drugs Coordinator and his Deputy report to HS(D). Their role on behalf of Ministers is to provide the day-to-day leadership and focus on implementing and developing the Government's strategy. The Coordinator will, in particular, scrutinise rigorously the performance of departments and agencies - individually and collectively - against the actions, objectives and performance indicators set out in this report; and produce a National Anti-Drugs Plan for implementation in each succeeding year. Departments will continue to be responsible for their own policies and resources, and accountable to their Ministers accordingly. But the Coordinator's responsibility to the Government for the production of his Annual Report and Plan, means that progress across the board will be coordinated and open to scrutiny.

To aid his role, the Coordinator will chair a new body named the UK Anti-Drugs Strategic Steering Group, which will meet regularly to help the Coordinator assess overall progress in implementing the strategy, including its resources; consider relevant developments in the rest of the UK and internationally; and plan to account for progress and the way forward via the Coordinator's Annual Report and Plan.

Representation on the Strategic Steering Group will include senior officials from within Government, and individuals from independent bodies, professional drug agencies, local government, business and Drug Action Teams.

The Deputy UK Anti-Drugs Coordinator will, in turn, take forward the key elements of this White Paper through four newly formed Strategy Support Groups - one group for each aim of the strategy, each group meeting regularly. The key tasks of these groups will be to monitor progress against each aim; assess the need for further support in its implementation; consider emerging training, research and information needs; and monitor resource implications. These groups will report back to the Steering Group.

The Coordinator's and Deputy's roles can only be effective through collaboration and involvement of a wide range of supportive groups and individuals. To this end they will have support from the UK Anti-Drugs Coordination Unit (previously known as the Central Drugs Coordination Unit), a Unit in the Privy Council Office, reporting to the President of the Council, whose funding arrangements will be put on a long-term basis.

The UKADCU's role will be to support the monitoring and effective implementation of this strategy. To fulfil this role, the UKADCU will work very closely with Departments, Drug Action Teams and individual agencies to develop a comprehensive network of resources and support mechanisms geared towards the strategy's implementation.

Resources

Government expenditure in tackling drug misuse is considerable but poorly coordinated. As a result of the work on drug-related spending carried out for the Comprehensive Spending Review, we know that total Government expenditure for 1997/98 was in the region of £1.4 billion. This big increase in estimated expenditure - compared to £500 million in 1993/94 - relates primarily to a more realistic assessment of the drugs related proportion of generic police/prison/probation/education/health activity. We estimate that 62% of this total is currently spent on enforcement related work, much of it reactive and not drugs-specific (eg police, court, probation and prisions) and therefore, not straightforwardly transferable to preventative programmes; 13% on treatment; 12% on prevention and education; and 13% on international supply reduction. No more than a third of that total expenditure is currently spent on preventing drug misuse (as opposed to coping with the consequences of the problem). Minimum estimated costs of the social problems generated by severely dependent drug misusers alone are in the region of £3-4 billion annually.

Existing resource provision is ad hoc rather than strategic; allocation mechanisms are largely historically driven; the pattern of the delivery of resources to local anti-drugs projects is complicated and random; efforts to realise substantial confiscated assets from drug-related activity have not previously been successful; and there has been a lack of clear coordination between objectives, resources and outcomes. In moving forward, it is clear that the Government's resources must be linked to this strategy.

An announcement on funding from 1999/2000 will be made later in the year, following the outcome of the Government's Comprehensive Spending Review. Reforms will be guided by the following principles:

- drug-related expenditure should over time shift away from reacting to the consequences of the drugs problem and towards positive investment in preventing and targeting it;

- the bulk of targeted resources should be spent on collaborative projects which tackle high priority groups - in particular vulnerable young people, drug-related offenders and problem drug misusers;

- resources for drug-specific activities should receive priority within health authorities budgets, and on the basis of partnership work wherever appropriate. **Health authorities** should be required to deliver this strategy through the NHS Priorities and Planning Guidance. The development of the new NHS and Public Health White Papers should be used to ensure that health authorities give adequate provision to meeting the aims of the strategy through central guidance. Health authorities will be expected to include anti-drugs measures in their Health Improvement Programme;

- an element should be identified within health authorities' drug allocation for developing specific young people's services. This should enable health authorities to develop services in line with Department of Health guidance;

- funding for the purchase of community care services for drug misusers should be given adequate priority by **local authorities** . The Department of Health should take steps to ensure that this money is used for drug-specific partnership work, with mechanisms put in place to ensure that current expenditure on drug misusers from local authority community care funding is protected;

- **police forces** should aim to direct resources from within their budgets to drugs-specific partnership work, with explicit priority given to this work in Police Authority Annual Policing plans and the national key policing objectives, set by the Home Secretary and performance indicators and targets aligned explicitly to the new strategy;

- the **Prison Service** should aim to direct resources from within their budget to drugs-specific partnership work, including treatment provision, with explicit priority given to this work in the Prison Service business plan, and performance indicators and targets aligned explicitly to the new strategy;

- **probation services** should aim to direct resources from within their budgets to drugs-specific partnership work, with explicit priority given to this work in local plans and the national key probation objectives, and performance indicators and targets aligned explicitly to the new strategy;

- **local education authorities** should include clear policy statements on drugs education, and any performance indicators and targets aligned to the new strategy, within their behaviour support plans. An LEA's anti-drugs strategy will also be reflected in its education development plan where this emerges as a priority;

- **HM Customs and Excise** should maintain their commitment to funding drug-related activity - and ensure that partnership work is reaffirmed strongly in their management plans, with performance indicators and targets aligned explicitly to the new strategy;

- the **National Criminal Intelligence Service** should ensure that partnership work is reaffirmed strongly in their service plan, and to consider in consultation with the Coordinator the development of objectives with performance indicators and targets aligned explicitly to the new strategy;

- the **National Crime Squad** should ensure that partnership work is reaffirmed strongly in their service plan, and to consider in consultation with the Coordinator the development of objectives with performance indicators aligned explicitly to the new strategy;

- **Drug Action Teams** should be the principal mechanism by which agencies will develop the resource partnerships outlined above, and will assess regularly whether the spending plans and projected outcomes of all agencies represented on them are aligned explicitly to the new strategy;

- the value for money of Government and other anti-drugs expenditure against outcomes should be monitored at national level via the UK Strategic Steering Group and Strategy Support Groups and locally via the Drug Action Teams; and

- securing partnership funding should be given high priority at every level, led by the national partnership between Government and Business in the Community;

For the first time, a proportion of assets seized from drug barons will be channelled back into anti-drugs programmes to help those who have suffered at their hands and on whose misfortune they have prospered. The Government is considering how this can best be achieved. More details of these considerations will be issued later this year.

The efficient and effective delivery of the strategy's objectives will, of course, determine the specific resources required over time, and resource provision will accordingly be regularly reviewed in the Coordinator's Annual Report and Plan of Action Against Drug Misuse.

Regional Coordination and Delivery of Strategy

Drug Action Teams, supported by their Reference Groups, have worked well in most parts of the country in forging partnerships against drugs amongst the key local agencies. The time is right to step up a gear in relation to this partnership activity, so that a sharper focus is brought to bear on implementing this strategy. This should link up where necessary with other local partnership initiatives on welfare-to-work, health, education, housing, community safety, youth justice, local democracy and social exclusion. Links with these other partnerships will develop over time, but will not diminish the importance of the work against drugs at local and regional level, via Drug Action Teams. The strategic requirements set out below reinforce both the need for a continuing focus on local drugs problems and ensuring that other social partnerships contribute to that work.

All Drug Action Teams in England are to agree corporate plans annually with the UK Anti-Drugs Coordinator by the end of each calendar year. Templates will be provided by UKADCU. These plans will feed into the Annual Report and Plan and include:

- an assessment of current progress against the new strategy;

- an analysis of existing local resources upon which each DAT has influence both within its own organisations and jointly targeted;

- proposals for allocating those resources to match the priority aims and actions set out in this strategy;

- specific outcome measures against all relevant areas under the aims set out in this strategy - including services for vulnerable young people, criminal justice/treatment; rehabilitation of problem drug misusers and disruption of local drug markets;

- proposals for short, medium and longer-term targets against those measures in line with the national targets to be developed;

- agreement with all other Drug Action Teams within their metropolitan or shire county area on the basis of a corporate and strategic overview to the plans individual DATs have drawn up. This is to ensure strategic coherence to the plans across each county, a genuinely senior level of strategic input from the key players, and consonance with the development of other relevant shire and metropolitan county partnerships. Where appropriate, DATs will wish to liaise with relevant regional tiers of government. **This overview will be the most important part of the plan in enabling the Coordinator to take stock of progress.** Those DATs which currently do not operate on a shire or metropolitan county level will have a more complex process to go through than the 26 DATs currently operating on those lines. The focus of our support will therefore be on the remaining 80 DATs.

These plans will deliver greater consistency and provide the basis for attracting additional resources - including some drugs-specific funding from central Government, Lottery funding and partnership money from the private and voluntary sectors - and will be assessed on that basis. The Government and the Coordinators will be engaging directly with Drug Action Teams across England to ensure that the planning process is as clear and unbureaucratic as possible.

Drug Action Teams must develop as the mechanism for ensuring local resource collaboration in line with this strategy. Their corporate plans will provide the benchmark for distributing resources from 1999/2000 onwards - further guidance to DATs will be provided later this year taking forward this challenging remit. This will include more information about the future of centrally provided development funding.

This funding has helped DATs in providing essential local coordination. Most DATs have demonstrated best value in using this resource through an identifiable coordinator, working closely to the DAT Chair, and with a clear role and set of requirements. This coordination role must include coherent representation to the DAT of the views and expertise available from local communities. The Chair of each Drug Action Team will continue to have overall responsibility for the formulation and implementation of corporate plans. Clearly that responsibility, which also entails some accountability to the Coordinator, can only be discharged by individuals with considerable authority and influence within their DAT area. The personal qualities of any individual Chair are far more significant than the agency from which they come.

Representation on DATs - beyond the core agencies of health authorities, education, social services, police, prisons and probation - will continue to be a local matter, with the exception that all DATs should include senior representatives from local authority housing. They should also liaise more closely with the Crown Prosecution Service, key sentencers, the Employment Service, the voluntary sector, Training and Enterprise Councils and Chambers of Commerce. DATs must also actively engage their elected members and Members of Parliament, to ensure that there is no "democratic deficit" to their activity. Developing the representation and function of Drug Reference Groups and other networks in support of the agreed plans of the Drug Action Teams will be a local matter, but will need to ensure effective community involvement, consultation networks and clarity of responsibilities for implementation.

Drug Action Teams or their equivalents in Scotland, Wales and Northern Ireland are invited to consider their own development in the light of this strategy, as part of the overall response to the Coordinator by February 1999.

Partnerships

Action against drugs problems cannot be undertaken effectively by any single agency. The performance of all statutory agencies, accountable to central Government Departments, will be scrutinised to assess their progress in forging effective, enduring and practical partnerships with other agencies. The following are being developed as a priority:

- **The FCO's Special Representative's** international coordination committee will continue under the Chairmanship of the Special Representative to ensure the strongest possible links with our European partners to give continuing effect to the leading role of the UK in the fight against drugs established during our Presidency of the EU from January to June 1998. The UK will also take a visible lead in international coordinated efforts against drugs, through the UN and other mechanisms, where that has a direct contribution to make to this strategy's vision. Our resources will be made available accordingly;

- **statutory Inspectorates** - each HM Inspectorate will continue to have direct responsibility for monitoring the impact of drugs policies for which their agencies are responsible. The importance of collaborative working across and beyond the Inspectorates is recognised by all of them. A multi-disciplinary review process - involving representatives from HM Inspectorate of Constabulary, HM Inspectorate of Prisons, HMI Probation, OFSTED and the Social Services Inspectorate - will be established by December 1998. The importance of monitoring health authorities in this context will need further examination;

- **national programme delivery** - the role of Government is to facilitate and enable this strategy's implementation through leadership and resource provision. In areas such as publicity, spreading of best practice, project programmes, information collation, and specialist guidance, there is already expertise and experience among a number of organisations, funded by Government or others. In view of its valuable contribution to date, it is planned that there should be some successor arrangements to the Home Office Drugs Prevention Initiative after its current programme ends in March 1999, which will support this strategy and promote community-based drugs prevention across England. Other bodies with a role to play include the Standing Conference on Drug Abuse, the Institute for the Study of Drug Dependence, Alcohol Concern, the Substance Misuse Advisory Service, the Local Government Drugs Forum and the Health Education Authority. To avoid unnecessary duplication of effort, any work the Government commissions in support of the vision, aims and actions set out in this strategy - contracted to one or more of these agencies - will only be provided on the basis of clear partnership agreements;

- **Advisory Council on the Misuse of Drugs** - the ACMD has the statutory responsibility to advise Government on the continuing operation of the Misuse of Drugs Act 1971, and to any changes to the law necessary in the light of emerging evidence. The Council will continue to exercise that vital function. In addition, the Council has produced many extremely valuable reports on specific issues - most recently on drugs and the environment which will be published soon. Its composition and focus of work need to be harnessed as closely as possible to the thrust of this long-term strategy and to the work of the Coordinator, and its future work priorities will evolve in that context;

- **private sector** - the private sector plays a vital role at national, regional and local level in working to combat drug misuse. Many businesses now recognise the commercial benefits and ethical imperatives of involvement in this work. Some - such as BT, Boots, Proctor and Gamble, Marks & Spencer, Royal and Sun Alliance, McDonald's, Lloyds TSB - have already contributed significant resources and commitment to this work. Business in the Community is driving forward a major strategy programme to engage the private sector as systematically as possible - especially through initiatives aimed at young people;

- **voluntary sector** - much of the energy and innovation in tackling drug misuse, as well as professional and cost-effective delivery, comes from the voluntary sector. We are determined to maximise the contributions that this sector can make set against this strategy. The UK Anti-Drugs Coordinator will convene an annual national stocktake of voluntary sector providers, in concert with the Standing Conference on Drug Abuse, to ensure that their interests and contributions to the developing strategy are fully developed and properly used, and that best practice is being implemented;

- **the media** - responsible and informed coverage of drugs stories can make an important contribution to the strategy's vision. We will engage extensively with national, regional and local media to try to ensure a good level of informed debate, analysis and coverage;

- **parents/young people/communities** - drugs impact on all of us, our lives, worries and aspirations. We will consult and engage with people in schools, clubs, at parents meetings, with users, at community events and in all locations where there is real concern and real commitment to addressing it.

Audit and Evaluation

Objective and rigorous assessment of the effectiveness of implementing this strategy will be a central feature of its development, and necessary adjustments will be made as a consequence. The key components of this process will be as follows:

- the Coordinator's Annual Report and Plan of Action Against Drug Misuse which will be published every Spring, based on the strategic framework set out here, together with data on progress and proposals for future priorities;

- annual reports from Drug Action Teams in England made to the Coordinator - these will be submitted as part of the corporate planning process at the end of each calendar year. Results and best practice will be incorporated into the Coordinator's Annual Report and Plan;

- the statutory Inspectorates - regular thematic and multi-disciplinary reviews will be published by these bodies;

- quality indicators for the core statutory agencies - these will reflect the fact that the quantitative indicators to be set out need harnessing to more qualitative assessments of progress, which will form part of the DAT reporting process at local level and of an overview from the Coordinator's Annual Report and Plan;

- research and information - this will be regularly assessed against each of the strategy's four aims by the four strategy support groups, as an integral part of the implementation process. They will consult a wide range of external bodies as necessary, and report collectively to the Strategic Steering Group;

- independent strategic evaluation - over the longer term, we will all need to be satisfied that the implementation of this strategy is achieving the most effective results possible. The National Audit Office and the Audit Commission will be engaged in discussions about what might be undertaken over the next decade to fulfil this remit;

- consultations - the continual process of "listening and learning" which the Coordinator and his Deputy have undertaken from day one, will form a more informal, but essential, part of evaluating the strategy. They will continue this consultation for the rest of their appointments, so that progress on the ground - where it really matters - can be properly assessed.

Designed and produced by Sovereign Design (0171 740 4010) for the
Central Drugs Coordination Unit (SD1000)

Printed in the UK for The Stationery Office Limited on behalf of the Controller of Her Majesty's Stationery Office
Dd 8459989, 4/98, 77240